The Wildlife

and how to find it
by
Jay Butler and Anna Levin

Publishers' Introduction.

One September day, armed with the suggestions and tips offered in this guide, the publishers set out to test drive the wildlife car trip described on page 29. Along the shores of Loch na Keal, we saw a bird far out on the water that, on another day, would only have rated the mental note "probably a gull." But today we doing it by the book, so the car was stopped, the fieldglasses went up and the distant bird was identified as a guillemot. This, in itself, was a nice tick for the day's list, but this guillemot was behaving in a strange fashion, paddling furiously, shaking its head and quite clearly very agitated. A little more patient watching enabled us to see that it had a truly enormous fish in its beak. This fish was not far short of its own length and it was attempting to swallow it. For some reason, a main part of the bird's strategy seemed to lie in paddling furiously forwards, creating a wake like a miniature steamer and forging through the water at such a speed that its by now totally fascinated watchers had to drive slowly along the road to keep up. Other cars passed us and overtook us, all oblivious to the stirring drama taking place off shore. We must have been there half an hour, unable to tear ourselves away until, at last, the bird dived. When it came up again, the fish had gone. We saw other things that day – more seabirds, several buzzards and deer in the gloaming. But the little guillemot was the wildlife experience of the day. All because we had stopped, got out the fieldglasses and given ourselves time to watch and learn.

Thank you Jay and Anna.

Brown & Whittaker
2003
Reprinted 2007

Country code

Gates

Farmers say that when walkers cross their land, gates cause more problems than anything else, so we would ask, on their behalf, that you respect these rules: if you find a gate open, leave it open; if you find a gate closed, shut it after you again, securely fastened and stockproof; if you find a gate locked or tied up with string or wire, please don't try to open it. Climb it at the hinge end.

Dogs

Dogs also cause problems for farmers so we would ask you to keep your dog under control where there are animals and to take special note of the lambing season (March to May) when sheep should not be disturbed. If you find any animal in distress such as an apparently lost lamb or a sheep stuck on a ledge, report it, do not attempt to deal with it yourself.

Go carefully on single track roads. The passing places are for vehicles to pass or to allow overtaking. Never park there or anywhere where it is likely to cause difficulty of access to farmers' fields.

Respect wildlife, plants and trees, and guard against fire.

Leave no litter.

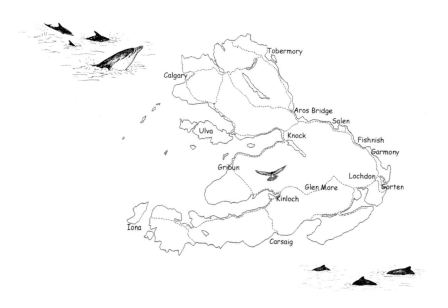

Contents

Text and illustrations © Jay Butler and Anna Levin 2003
Published by Brown & Whittaker Publishing, Tobermory, Isle of Mull, PA75 6PR
Printed by Nevisprint Ltd, Fort William
ISBN 0 9532775 2 6
ISBN 9780953277520

Spotting Tips

What to take & wear: This book! Binoculars and chocolate. Wear warm clothes, preferably soft greens or browns and avoid noisy or rustling garments.

When to watch: Although you can see wildlife at any time of day, dusk and dawn are, for many creatures, times of increased activity and therefore good for dedicated watching. Intermittent showers can be great for bird watching because when the rain stops, birds will fly into wind to dry their feathers.

Sound: Whispering voices actually carry much further than you think, and so when out with others try using sign language instead. By deciding on signals before you set out, communicating with sign language can be really fun. Avoid walking on twigs as the cracks and crunches will send surrounding creatures diving for cover. Don't stomp along chatting to your companions in the hope that some creature will just present itself to you. Move slowly and quietly, making frequent stops just to look and listen. In a group stay close together and if you have seen something and want to get closer, try to move smoothly as if your group is one single object not separate individuals. This can be achieved quite easily by walking in each other's steps and keeping in time to reduce the overall noise.

Scent: Animals have extremely good noses and will whiff a molecule of Calvin Klein miles off, and so if moving in close to an animal, check that the wind is blowing your scent AWAY, so that you are downwind of your quarry.

Sight: Most animals are acutely aware of their surroundings and will quickly pick out anything that should not be there. Once out in the open, you become very conspicuous so try to keep next to natural objects larger than yourself so that you melt into the surrounding landscape. Where possible keep below the skyline and if you see anything — stop and keep very still and just wait. Most animals, including humans, seldom look up, and so gaining a position of height can be an excellent way of watching without being seen.

Watching at night: Many creatures are only active after dark and because of this are difficult to see. A useful trick is to paint the bulb of your torch with layers of red felt-tip pen. Such a device can be used very effectively to illuminate animals without disturbing them. Be careful though, you can deceive an animal's eyes by using a red filter but not its ears or nose!

Safety: If you plan to spend the day in a remote location check the weather; take a map, whistle, torch and some food and drink. Most importantly always tell someone where you are going and when you expect to return.

Lolling Lumps

Both grey and common seals are a familiar sight around Mull's rocky coastline and of all the island's mammals they are the easiest to spot. Apart from during the mating season (September–December) **grey seals** spend most of their time at sea and so in the summer months you are most likely to see the smaller, rounder **common seal**.

Seals rest by hanging vertically in the water — a pose know as bottling. With their noses pointed skywards, their heads appear cone shaped. When the snooze is over, the dome of the head can be seen melting back into the water. From a distance, or perhaps from the roadside at Salen Bay or Loch na Keal, look carefully out to the skerries (rocks). Look for long, light shapes among the dark, kelp-draped rocks. Common seals often bask with their heads raised and bodies arched so if you see a greyish banana shape, you are probably looking at a head up, tail up, hauled-out seal.

As both grey and common seals are of a similar size and colour, it is often difficult to distinguish between the two species. If you can get close enough, the difference in their profiles will help identify them. Face on, the nostrils of the common seal form a distinctive 'V' shape and the head is round and small, whereas grey seals have larger heads, sporting rolls of flesh at the neck, and 'W' shape nostrils across the end of their distinctly Roman noses. Unlike greys, common seals are quiet, placid creatures so if you hear any barking, hissing or snarling it is most likely to be a grey.

Water Wise

While otters are indigenous to the island, the **mink** on Mull are descended from fur farm escapees. They are now present in such high numbers that one can be found along every kilometre of Mull's coastline. Each individual mink defends its own territory within which it hunts. Being adept swimmers they can easily access the islands on sheltered lochs and firths where sea birds breed in dense colonies that would otherwise be safe from ground predators. Their effect on these colonies is devastating as they kill indiscriminately, wiping out eggs and chicks which can result in a total breeding failure. Indeed, the largest colony of common terns in Britain, which is just off Craignure, has seriously been endangered by the mink and now requires protection.

Mink and otter both belong to the same family and are often confused with each other. However, mink are actually shorter, thinner and faster than otters. Their movement takes on a more scurrying nature on land and they are neat and angular when swimming. When startled, their sharp, pointed little faces often stop and stare defiantly back at the intruder.

If you take a minute to think about the type of creatures they are, distinguishing between them becomes easier. Mink are primarily land animals that are extremely efficient swimmers, while otters are primarily aquatic creatures that are content on land. This is clearly reflected in their respective body movements. When mink are in the water, they tend to be rather business-like, intent on getting from A to B for a distinct purpose, usually food. Whereas swimming otters are in their element and tend not to spend much time actually swimming but rather rolling, lolling, diving and playing. With their graceful, fluid movements they seem to relish any opportunity just to *be* in the water.

The north and west coasts of Scotland hold the largest population of **otters** in Europe, and Mull is an excellent place to capitalise on this. An evening walk along low, rocky shores may well pay dividends to the keen otter spotter.

One way to determine if otters are around is to look for a 'spraint' (otter poo to you and me), often deposited conscientiously on the highest part of a rock or boulder. Quite often you will find such higher rocks below bridges, this is a favourite toilet spot and always worth checking. This apparently odd choice of toilet location is actually an important part of their behaviour. By positioning the spraint as high as possible, the scent, which informs intruders who is the rightful owner of that particular stretch of water, carries further.

As they tend to be extremely shy, the chances of seeing an otter really close-up are remote. The skill is in knowing what to look for — from a distance otters can bear an uncanny resemblance to Loch Ness monsters. They move along the shore with undulating gait, back arched and thick, chunky tail usually carried in a 'U' shape. When swimming, the tail extends flat behind them and often flicks up before diving.

Going Batty

Collectively, bats are one of the most endangered species in Britain. Their two main needs, food and shelter, are both threatened by modern farming practices. The intense cultivation of arable crops means that old hollow trees and hedges are removed resulting in the destruction of the bats' shelter. Worse, the crop spraying involved in large-scale cultivation not only decimates the insects that bats feed on, but the accumulation of poison in their bodies eventually kills them. However, the good news is that, as with most Hebridean islands, intensive arable farming is not practiced on Mull, which means there is an abundance of bat-friendly habitats on the island. Indeed, Mull is home to four species of bat: Daubenton's, Natterer's, common long-eared and the tiny pipistrelle. To the untrained eye, and without the help of such gizmos as modern bat detectors, you are unlikely to be able to confidently identify the different species. However, the pointers below should help.

The tiny **pipistrelle** bat is not only the smallest but also the most abundant and widespread bat in Britain, and Mull has its fair share of these lovely little creatures. Large numbers live together and they can sometimes be heard squeaking excitedly a few minutes before streaming out en masse from their roosting place to find food in the early evening. From a distance, this early evening dispersal resembles a cloud of pepper on a puff of wind.

Dervaig, Tobermory and Aros Park are good places to see pipistrelle bats as they dip and dive in the dusk. They often make their homes in the warm, comfortable roofs of Tobermory houses.

Principally a woodland dweller, the **common long-eared** bat, as
its name would suggest, has magnificent oval ears that are nearly three
quarters of the combined length of its head and body. These bats are
nimble flyers and may be seen threading their way through pockets of
woodland and hovering upright over insect laden leaves. Although their favoured
roosts are hollow trees, they also often take up residence in houses.

As all Mull's bats hibernate during the winter, summer is the time to go bat
spotting. Some good areas to try are the castles at Duart, Torosay and the
ruins of Aros. Salen is also a good place to spot them.

Natterer's bats like coniferous plantations, of which there are many on Mull,
and are often seen in slow flight around them. They roost in hollow trees, caves
and buildings — particularly castles. Adult females form large nursery colonies
containing between 100 and 200 bats. They come out to feed about an hour
after sunset and don't return until an hour or two before sunrise.

Daubenton's bats also enjoy the ambience of castles, but failing that they will
take up residence in a cosy tree or cave, usually close to water. At dusk they
can be seen skimming low over ponds or lochs where they feed on mayflies,
plankton and sometimes even small fish.

9

On your doorstep

It is not only in the wild and remote locations that you can find wildlife on Mull, it is everywhere. Right on your doorstep, close to human dwellings, there is an abundance of interesting wildlife. So wherever you are staying make a conscious effort to really look around.

Slow worm

These serpent-like reptiles are actually not worms or snakes but legless lizards. As avid slug eaters, these harmless little creatures are an asset to any garden.

Although unhurried and deliberate movers they have a surprising turn of speed when the need arises — probably just as well as they are often snacked upon by hedgehogs, adders, rats, kestrels, frogs and toads. Slow worms are known to live longer than any other lizard — one in captivity actually made it into its fifties.

Mole

Moles perform all their daily routines below ground in an extensive burrow system and, with the exception of the mating season, lead a completely solitary life.

Their spade-like feet and strong claws make them well adapted to their subterranean lifestyle. The burrow provides not only accommodation but also their favourite food — earthworms, which are sometimes cached *alive* in special larders within their burrows. One such larder was discovered to contain a staggering 1,280 earthworms and 18 grubs! The earthworms are bitten in such a way as to keep them alive, but immobilised. A mole requires the equivalent of half its own body weight in food each day and this gruesome but ingenious behaviour provides the mole with an abundance of fresh food to see it through cold, hard winters.

House mouse

As their name suggests, these little fellows are most often found in or close to buildings and although they can live independently of humans, they are best known for taking up residence where food or grain is stored. Their decidedly wasteful eating habits make their presence easy to identify. So if you come across an array of crumbs, husks and half-eaten morsels you can be pretty sure a house mouse has been dining in the vicinity. They are particularly fond of living in the crevices of dry stone walls where, in the early evening, they may be seen squeezing their round little bodies into the tiniest of cracks. Their tails serve to regulate their body heat — the colder the climate, the shorter the tail. Kestrels, hawks, polecats and mink will all happily dine on house mice.

Hedgehog

If you go out after dark with a torch and search in moist, grassy areas you may well come across this short, rotund, spiny little chap snuffling around. Hedgehogs are often seen in gardens lined by good thick hedges, within which they will live. Their sharp spines make them an unattractive food source to most creatures but they are sometimes taken by polecats, owls and even eagles.

Hedgehogs have a mysterious habit of anointing themselves with masses of their own frothy saliva, which they plaster all over their spiny body with their long, pink tongues.

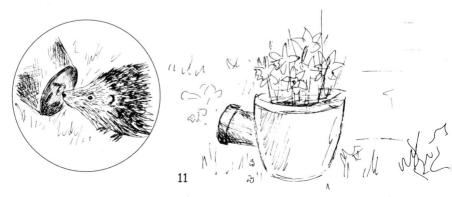

Dinner page

The creatures mentioned here are not glamorous — indeed shrews are unlikely to feature in the tourist board marketing strategy for the island, but these diminutive creatures are crucial to the rich and varied ecology of Mull. The many raptors we have here thrive because of the abundance of these wee beasties.

So while you scan the skies in the hope of spotting some of Mull's magnificent raptors, spare a thought for those upon which their existence depends. Listen, for example, for the sound of voles chittering in the long grass and look for their oval-shaped tunnels and runs. Such clues confirm that creatures are scuttling around in the undergrowth, and you can be sure that raptors will soon be hunting there!

Field/short-tailed vole

Mull's extensive grassland habitat is home to a very large number of voles, which are reported to be substantially larger than their mainland counterparts. Once again you are unlikely to actually see a field vole as they are tiny and live their entire lives in runs below rough grass. Get down and lift up grassy tussocks and if you see little tunnels — well-formed runways rounded in the dense grass — stand still and listen. Especially in early evenings during late summer when they are most vocal, you may well hear them chittering and squeaking at each other. The humble field vole is the primary source of food for barn owls (making up an incredible 90 per cent of their diet) and is also considered a delicacy by herons, eagles, owls and stoats, to name but a few.

Wood mouse

Not just woodland, but a wide variety of habitats, including farmland, open grassland and heather are home to the wood mouse.

They dig numerous runs that form miniature subterranean villages which are often associated with small trees, usually hazel. Around the base of these trees you may see the tell tale holes of the tunnel entrances. Some of the tunnels end in nesting chambers, usually lined with leaves, moss and grass and it is here that the young are born.

Just off this 'nursery' another tunnel leads to a mouse 'kitchen', usually well stocked with cached food. Wood mice are themselves food for a variety of predators and curiously when frightened, stop whatever they were doing in favour of vigorously grooming their armpits!

Shrew

Although there are three species of shrew on Mull (water, pygmy and common), you are unlikely to see them as they are small, fast and mostly active at night. These creatures are aggressive and pugnacious to each other at all times. On meeting, individuals freeze before rearing up on their hind legs and squeaking loudly. If one retreats, a chase ensues, sometimes resulting in a violent scuffle, where the sole aim is to decapitate the opponent, or failing that, bite its tail off! With the exception of spring, when they mate and rear young, they are, not surprisingly, entirely solitary.

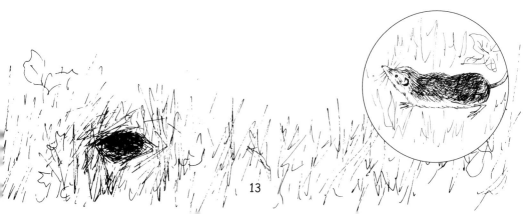

Ghosts of the night

Silent and ghostly with a pale, heart-shaped face, the **barn owl** can be seen gliding silently over grass and moorland in search of rats, mice and voles. In early spring, these owls return to favoured nesting sites such as old barns, ruins and sometimes tree cavities. On Mull, barn owls also nest in caves.

Owls take their prey whole and the indigestible remnants, such as bone and fur, form smooth, tightly packed cylinders in the throat. These are then spat out below the roosting site and finding these dark, shiny, oval pellets is an excellent way to confirm the presence of owls. The UK population of barn owls, which are a protected species, is estimated at only 4,000 pairs. With 16 recorded breeding pairs on the island, it is clear that Mull's barn owl population is of vital importance and as such is closely protected.

Although extremely scarce, **long-eared owls** are present in the south of Mull. With perfect camouflage they roost during the day in inaccessible dense coniferous woodland, but do hunt at night in the open. If disturbed when nesting, the female will attempt to frighten away the intruder by raising her wings to frame her enormous face.

Tawny owls are widespread on Mull and are often seen on or close to roads. They are found in woodland and farmland and sometimes also take up residence in large gardens. They have dark brown faces, big dark eyes and their call is the familiar 'hoo-hoo-hooooo' often described as 'to-whit-to-wooo'.

With wing beats like a gigantic moth, the more abundant **short-eared owl** can be seen throughout the island patrolling low over open grassland. Using their acute sense of hearing rather than sight, they listen for the tell tale rustling of mice and voles. Their pronounced yellow eyes are surprisingly visible even when flying.

Raunchy Raptors

With its abundance of mountain top wilderness, extensive moorland, and coniferous woodland, Mull is able to provide a variety of raptors with the habitats so crucial to their survival. Featuring high on the guest list we find:- goshawks, sparrowhawks, peregrine falcons, kestrels, hen harriers, merlins, buzzards and, of course, the stars of the show — the eagles.

Terrified small birds will scatter like dust in the wind before the needle-sharp talons of the agile and deadly **sparrowhawk**. The short, strong, rounded wings afford this jet-fighter pilot of the bird world the speed and agility to pursue its prey close to the ground through dense woodland, out-manoeuvring the intended victim with every twist and turn.

Also in search of woodland feasts is the **goshawk** which closely resembles the sparrowhawk with its pale barred underparts and darker wing surfaces. Females, approaching buzzard size, are much larger than males. With superb control, they swoop through the trees, taking larger birds and sometimes even rats and hares.

The most widespread of all British
falcons is the chestnut-coloured **kestrel** and
its familiar roadside hover needs little introduction. In Mull's rich
grassland habitat, kestrels are not restricted to roadside verges as they
often are on the mainland and may be seen just as often hunting over open
spaces. Even from a distance, the rapid, fluttering wing movements of the
hover are unmistakably kestrel. Watch, as from the hover they drop like a
stone, then momentarily stop in mid-air as if hauled up by an invisible length
of rope then down again for the kill.

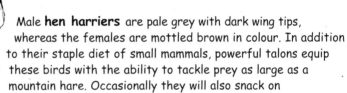

Male **hen harriers** are pale grey with dark wing tips,
whereas the females are mottled brown in colour. In addition
to their staple diet of small mammals, powerful talons equip
these birds with the ability to tackle prey as large as a
mountain hare. Occasionally they will also snack on
lizards, frogs and snakes but are little threat to the farmyard
hen that centuries ago earned them their name. They can be
seen hunting mostly over the gentle moorlands on the north
of the island. In the breeding season, the male flies
over the nest, with a prey offering, calling to
his mate. The female responds by flying up
towards him and, in a strange ritual,
turns herself upside down to catch the
offering as it is dropped.

Little bigger than a thrush, and often difficult to spot, the **merlin** is a fast, low-flying falcon, which feeds primarily on mice, lizards and small birds. Females are brown and males are blue-grey with a black tail band. In the mating season, the male will take a recently captured small bird off to a fence or wall — known as a 'plucking post' — where the victim is thoroughly plucked before being presented to its mate. Merlins can be seen on the Ross of Mull and also to the north in Dervaig.

Another deadly killer is the **peregrine falcon**, which circles high above its prey before snapping back its wings and plummeting, at speeds of up to 180mph, toward its unsuspecting victim. The blow usually shatters the victim's neck and death is instantaneous. To the ground-level observer, the whole incident is over in a flash and the only evidence remaining of the aerial carnage will be the silent, undulating passage of a few feathers as they float gently down to earth. On Mull, peregrines breed mainly on cliff sites and can be spotted on the west of the island.

High Flyers

The **sea eagle**, or white-tailed eagle, was once seen throughout Scotland but was driven to extinction through habitat loss and direct persecution. By the beginning of the 1900's only a few remained and the last recorded sighting was on Skye in 1916. A reintroduction programme began in the 1970s, bringing birds from Norway to the Isle of Rum. This programme has been successful and these awesome giants are now spreading through the Hebrides to resume their rightful place as the largest birds in Britain.

Sea eagles are now often seen on Mull. These magnificent birds with their strong, chunky wings are even larger than golden eagles. They can be readily distinguished by their white tails and extraordinarily rectangular flight profile, which may be described as closely resembling a wardrobe door in flight! Indeed their wingspan, at over two metres, is actually bigger than a standard door. They feed on carrion, seabirds, mammals and fish, and it is said that if you see the remains of a carcass scattered over a large area, the culprit is likely to have been a sea eagle.

With a majesty above all other raptors, the **golden eagle** is the bird that people most often identify with the Scottish Highlands. To watch an eagle with its effortless mastery of the skies is a truly breathtaking experience. With unhurried supremacy, eagles claim ownership of their territories by soaring high in ever-widening circles until they eventually disappear into the clouds. In the regions of high ground such as Dun da Ghaoithe, Ben Buie and Creach Beinn, eagles can be so well camouflaged against the russet and gold of the mountains, that the first hint you may have of their presence is when a huge chunk of mountain appears to lift skyward. They feed mainly on rabbits and hares but will also take carrion. As buzzards are often mistaken for eagles the following tips should help in the correct identification. Eagles are seen almost exclusively in wild mountainous regions. Their exceptionally high soaring flight — with pronounced finger-like wingtips — can appear to be almost flapless. They are often accompanied by ravens who are quick to cash in on the eagle's kill. Even from a considerable distance, the eagle's head size is notably larger than that of a buzzard. Finally, eagles never sit on telegraph poles!

Today, the buzzard is Britain's most common large bird of prey and can be seen all over Mull. Keep an eye on the telegraph poles along the road sides as you are very likely to see the upright, bulky shape of a perching **buzzard**, the tell-tale whitish marking around its neck like a mayor's 'chain of office'. If you do see one while driving, resist the temptation to stop beside the bird as it will simply fly off.

Although their favourite prey species is rabbit, buzzards are tremendous opportunists and will eat almost anything including worms and carrion. Indeed, buzzards are sometimes seen waiting by mole hills, ready to snap up the worms forced to the surface by the tunnelling activity below.

Legging it

It is not the familiar brown hare but the **mountain hare** that lives on Mull, dwelling in well secluded, scraped out hollows high up the mountainside. When they emerge they move downhill to nibble on the sweeter lowland heathers and grasses, supplemented, on occasions, with their own soft droppings. During the summer, their fur is light brown but with the approach of winter they moult and the fur takes on a mottled appearance. In particularly hard winters, a third moult occurs and the fur turns completely white.

Mountain hares, although a little smaller than their brown counterparts, are magnificent, powerful creatures with pronounced hind legs and long ears. Generally speaking, the sheer bulk, as opposed to size, of a hare is unmistakable and if you are not sure whether you have seen a hare or a rabbit — it was not a hare! When disturbed, they don't 'bounce' like rabbits but streak off like a bullet with frequent, sharp, angular turns intended to confuse the pursuer.

Significantly smaller than hares, **rabbits** have always been a common sight around Mull. They live in large family groups, and occupy complex, multi-layered burrow systems known as warrens. As we write this, Mull's rabbit population is struggling to recover from a devastating viral disease, which occurred in the late 1990's. Although numbers on the Ross of Mull are now almost back to normal, they remain low elsewhere on the island. As rabbits are the primary food source for raptors, particularly eagles and buzzards, this reduction in numbers has had a significant effect on their predator species. This is highlighted by accounts of eagles resorting to the predation of sea birds and further emphasises the fragile nature of island ecology.

Introduced to Britain from the Continent in the 12th century, rabbits used to be considered an important part of the rural economy and a valuable source of meat and skins. Today however, despite being the food source that ensures the presence of some of our most spectacular raptors, rabbits are considered a major agricultural pest. When threatened they thump their hind legs on the ground as a warning and if the jaws or talons of a predator are simply too close for comfort, rabbits are known to emit a piercing squeal. It is thought that this serves to give the dinner-seeking predator such a shock that it drops the rabbit, thereby providing just enough time for escape.

Sleek and Savage

Of the sleek and savage brigade, only ferrets, stoats and polecats live on Mull — there are no weasels. Due to their similar size, shape and behaviour, polecats, ferrets and stoats are frequently confused with each other. This is not surprising as they all belong to the same family of carnivores known as Mustelidae (as indeed do badgers, mink and otters).

So how do we distinguish between them? **Stoats** have russety-brown coats and are slightly smaller than ferrets. They are often seen standing on their hind legs, their sharp, pointed little faces raised high as they try to pick up a scent trail that will signify their next meal. In this posture the soft, white belly and dark-tipped tail, held upwards, can be used as instant confirmation of identity.

True **polecats** have a dark coat and a strikingly light face with a dark eye mask that is easily distinguishable. Their appetite for breeding with domestic ferrets, which have no mask, pink eyes and are creamy-white in colour, has led to some debate about the purity of the strain on Mull. This is a shame as Mull was once regarded as the Scottish bastion of the polecat. Today you are more likely to see the result of this inbreeding — the **polecat-ferret**, which has a slight, but not pronounced, face mask and a light brown coat giving it a washed out, faded appearance. Both stoats and polecats are opportunists when it comes to food and will devour almost anything that comes their way, such as fruit, worms and even the odd frog. However their favoured prey is undoubtedly rabbits and as a result they are often found living close to large rabbit populations, sometimes even occupying deserted burrows.

Sun Seekers

Faint rustles as scampering feet scurry through the
undergrowth is often the first indication of the
presence of the **common lizard**, a familiar reptilian
inhabitant of Mull. Like adders, common lizards
hibernate through the winter, emerging in the spring to
seek out a mate. These agile, sharp-clawed little lizards
feed on a variety of small creatures particularly spiders and
are themselves a food source for adders, kestrels, rats and
birds. However, the ability to shed their tails when seized provides an effective
escape and deprives many a would-be consumer of its intended banquet. Both
adders and lizards are cold-blooded creatures and need the sun's warmth to
heat their bodies up to a point where they can go about their daily business —
which is why you may often see them sunbathing on warm rocks and sunny
slopes.

The **adder**, the most widespread snake in the UK — and the only snake on
Mull — can be distinguished by the dark, zigzag line along the length of its body,
coupled with a distinctive 'V' on the back of its head. Although venomous, adders
are timid creatures and will normally flee long before any human could get close
enough to provoke them into biting. During the winter they hibernate, often in
groups, in rock crevices or underground burrows.

As with most snakes, adders periodically shed their skins and such 'casts' can
be found around the Mishnish Lochs, and also on the appropriately named 'snake
pass' road below the lochs — both favourite haunts of Mull adders.

The extensive moorland on Mull is an ideal habitat for the adder, providing
shelter and an abundance of small mammals to snack on. Using heat sensors on
their snouts and forked tongues to pick up scent, adders pursue their victims
with icy precision. One bite from the hollow fangs through which venom is
injected and dinner is ready.

23

Domestic Bliss

Two breeds of sheep are farmed on Mull:- the **black-faced Linton** and the **Cheviot** both of which are tough and well able to survive harsh Highland winters. The black-faced is thought to have been brought to Britain by the Vikings and, along with the Cheviot, it was the sheep of the Highland clearances, when families were turned off the land to make way for flocks.

Sheep are very much an integral part of both Mull's history and economy. It was the introduction of sheep, over two centuries ago, that led to the vast expanses of moorland we see today. Contrary to popular belief, this landscape is not a natural cover but is in fact a direct result of the way sheep graze. Unlike cattle, sheep crop the grass extremely low. Their insatiable nibbling prevents regeneration, leaving a barren land devoid of wild flowers and trees. Indeed, some attribute the high density of midges, so prevalent in the Highlands, to the lack of bog myrtle — a known midge repellent, which has been decimated by sheep grazing.

However, it is these wild and bare mountain landscapes that support many of Mull's raptors, emphasising once again how this fascinating ecology is both interconnected and interdependent.

Visitors to the island often wonder why it is that the sheep are found roaming free and wrongly assume that they are escapees. Flocks are actually 'hefted' to certain regions of land — generation after generation will remain grazing just those areas. Sheep often lie on the roads soaking up the warmth of the heated tarmac. Approach with care as they do have a tendency to wait until the very last minute before deciding to get up and run out in front of your car.

As direct descendents of the Celtic Ox, **Highland cattle** are renowned for being the hardiest of all cattle breeds. With their long horns and thick, red coats, they bear an uncanny resemblance to woolly mammoths. But despite their fearsome appearance, they are actually — with the exception of mothers with young calves — noted for their docile nature.

Highland cattle take three to four years to mature and produce the fine-grained and well-flavoured lean beef for which they are renowned. The herds on Mull are an important part of the island's economy, as well as being an extremely popular tourist attraction.

If, like many visitors to Mull, you find your road to the ferry blocked by a group of unhurried, very horned cattle who are showing no indication of moving, try rustling an empty plastic bag out of the window as you move forward slowly. Failing that, a gentle but confident clapping of hands out of the window often gets them moving. They don't generally take kindly to horn blowing and bellowing — this is taken as an insult and can result in a swift, often damaging kick, or produce an even greater desire to continue their occupation of that exact spot.

The Roaring Rut

Scotland has very few of the elegant **fallow deer** that were once the favoured quarry of medieval huntsmen and are now most often associated with the parks of southern England. Although Mull's fallow deer population is small, they are quite easy to find as they remain localised to the area to which they were first introduced — the Gruline estate. One of the best places to spot fallow deer is just before the bridge at Knock. Although they can be seen at any time, dawn and dusk are the most likely spotting times, as during the day they tend to rest in secluded woodland.

In the summer, fallow deer have chestnut-brown coats with the classic (Bambi) white spots, but in wild herds, such as those on Mull, there can be considerable colour variations. Only the males (bucks) have antlers which, in contrast to red deer, are broad bladed, thick and appear less treacherous. Despite this, males in the mating season — or the rut as it is more commonly known — can do considerable damage to each other. With inspired ferocity, individual bucks charge each other head-on in an attempt to gain supremacy over their chosen group of females (does). During the mating season, which runs from October to November, the sound of clashing antlers can be heard for considerable distances.

The **red deer** is the UK's largest native mammal and has been a Highland inhabitant for over 20,000 years. They are magnificent beasts and may be found on many of Mull's wild moorland slopes. During the summer they tend to spend their time on the higher slopes feeding on grasses, heather and lichens but in the winter, and often at night, they move to lower ground where they can sometimes be seen near the roadside. Being exceptionally well-camouflaged against the brown and russet hillsides, they are difficult to see and more often than not, the first indication of their presence is a glimpse of fast-moving brown dots disappearing over the horizon. The best way to watch red deer is to try to keep upwind of them, ideally get a vantage point above them but without breaking the skyline.

Outside the mating season, stags (males) and hinds (females) do not mix, preferring to roam in single-sex herds. From a distance, a good way to determine whether you are viewing stags or hinds is to note their behaviour when disturbed: stags will scatter randomly whereas hinds will flee together.

During the rut, which runs from September to October, individual stags will fight each other to win the conjugal rights to a group of females. Males issue their challenges for this privileged access by bellowing and roaring. If you're walking through a valley on a misty autumnal day, you may well hear the eerie sound of this roaring, punctuated by the crack of interlocking antlers resonating down the mountain side.

In future years, Mull's population of red deer could become very special indeed. On the mainland red deer are crossbreeding with other species. Because of this, it is believed that the survival of the pure red deer species is in peril and that its existence will soon be limited exclusively to island populations.

Sure Feet

The shaggy **feral goat** has been in existence for well over 1,000 years and local folklore says that Mull's goat population is descended from goats that came ashore from Spanish galleons wrecked at the time of the Armada.

For most of the year, goats keep to high ground, wending their nimble-footed way around rocky coastal ledges. The groups tend to be small and discrete rather than scattered over a wide area and a favoured haunt is the cliffy south coast, especially along the route to Carsaig Arches. A visit to the cave and surrounding southern coastal areas may well be rewarded by a view of these primeval looking creatures.

These elusive animals can be surprisingly difficult to see and generally you are likely to detect the pungent aroma of goat, particularly the male, long before seeing them. Both sexes have backward-facing horns, which grow continually throughout their lives and in mature males can reach lengths of up to 76cm.

Suggested Excursions

The following excursions offer good opportunities for seeing the wildlife that lives on Mull. Here are three suggestions for a gentle walk, a more energetic walk and a drive to introduce you to Mull's varied habitats. These are only suggestions with some hints and tips that you can use anywhere else on the island.

Wildlife from your car

Although it is pleasant to go for a walk and see birds, animals and plants, it is just as easy to watch wildlife from your car. In fact, your car is an excellent 'hide' as it does not appear as a threat to most species.

This circuit will take you to different parts of Mull, and through different habitats, where you can use your spotting and recognition techniques to great advantage, while sitting in your car. Take along identification books and binoculars, and if you have a telescope, get a bracket which fits on your car window to keep it steady while you get a really close look at something.

This circuit can be joined at any point and done in either direction. Start at Aros Bridge where the road from Tobermory meets the road from Dervaig. Drive along the estuary in the direction of Salen and stop at the corner opposite Aros Castle where there is plenty of room to pull off the road. The best place is beside a ruined cottage where there is a bench. Scan the water and the shore for ducks and waders and start making a list of what you see. As you drive on along the road towards Salen, look out to the rocky island where you will definitely find seals – some will be lolling lumps and some will be in the head up, tail up, position. At very high tide the seals lie on the rocks which are just covered by the sea and look as if they are resting on the surface of the water. Can you decide if they are grey or common seals?

Drive into Salen and turn right at the church towards Gruline, crossing open country. Buzzards and other raptors are everywhere on Mull, and you might see some here. On the stretch between the sign for Macquarie's Mausoleum and the bridge at Knock there is a chance that you might catch a glimpse of fallow deer in the woods on either side, and perhaps some pheasants scurrying across the road. Continue along the shore of Loch na Keal and stop from time to time to look out to sea for a chance of a great northern diver, up in the hills for red deer, and high above for buzzards and possibly eagles. Keep stopping to look, to scan for movement, and if you get out of the car do it slowly and quietly. Slamming the doors is definitely not a good idea. You should now have got your eyes accustomed to noticing a quick splash in the water – a bird diving? an otter swimming? is it coming up again? Don't expect a diving bird or otter to come up exactly where it went down, so look around.

Highland and other cattle may be grazing in this area, and the sheep here spend all their lives out on the hill — except when they are dozing on a stretch of warm tarmac! Keep going slowly and steadily, and both cows and sheep will let you past. As you pass under the steep cliffs at Gribun look up for a sight of ravens, perhaps mobbing a bird of prey.

The road leaves the sea and starts to climb up and at the top it is fairly straight and level, passing through mountain and moorland — yet another type of habitat. Look out for deer on the hills on each side of the road, perhaps just breaking the skyline, or running in a herd. The road enters trees and it might now be time to find some running water and see if there are any dragonflies flitting about. Turn off to the right, about half a mile after entering the trees, and go down a few hundred yards. Stop just before a wooden bridge for a view down a small river. Look and listen for birds — perhaps some dippers in this habitat.

Coming down past the turn off to Tiroran, the road comes near the sea again — get the binoculars out to look for shore birds (how many herons have you seen so far?) or maybe an otter. Go on to the Kinloch junction, through open marshy ground that is typical hen harrier country. Turn left into Glen More and drive through this lonely glen — almost uninhabited by people these days, but with wild country that is home to red deer. When the hills become closer and higher, there is an old quarry on the right which is a place to park and scan the skyline for eagles soaring, often in pairs. When the weather clears after a shower of rain is a good time to see them take off and soar on the thermals. The quarry is of geological interest being the first of the Mull calderas — where magma burst through the Earth's crust, millions of years ago.

After Glen More, drive on towards Craignure, passing through more open country where deer are often grazing in the early morning or late evening. Next stop should be at Lochdon, one of the best places in Mull for shore birds. If you have time, make a diversion down to Gorten where there is room just before the farm gate for two or three cars to park. Your bird spotting list should rapidly get longer as you scan the shore and mud — as the tide comes in many birds work up the shore, feeding ahead of the advancing water. Curlew, Greenshank and Ringed Plover are among the species to expect here.

Pass through Craignure and on back towards Salen. This is a fairly dull part but has that special habitat preferred by Mull buzzards — telegraph poles — so you should be sure of seeing more than one. Turn off beside the cemetery at Pennygown and down behind the old graveyard wall where it is possible to get out of the car, and where there is a chance of seeing a school of dolphins passing up the Sound of Mull. From there back to the starting point at Aros Bridge - the seals are still on the rocks but the tide will be different.

Carsaig Walk (full day trip)

To experience nearly all the elements of Mull's natural history, the walk to the Carsaig Arches cannot be bettered. The publishers, asked by the authors to test these walks, in two separate excursions to Carsaig ticked all but one of the species mentioned (the rabbit!).

Everything starts with geology and here you can see how the island of Mull, built mainly of tertiary volcanic rocks, sits on a bed of much older rocks. Here, and in a few other places in Mull, the basement rocks appear under the skirts of the volcanics and because they have been constantly eroded by the relentless sea, the land above falls down steeply and dramatically into the Firth of Lorne forming a rampart of steep, unstable and very wildlife-friendly cliffs.

Park the car near the pier at Carsaig and, before setting off, take your binoculars down onto the pier for a quick scan for seabirds and seals. Once embarked on the walk, you may find that the stupendous cliffs draw the eye so irresistibly that it is easy to forget to look out over the sea to check for a fin breaking the surface or to glance down to the shore for a sighting of an otter clambering out to enjoy a quick nap behind a boulder.

Once across the head of Carsaig bay, the route runs through Jurassic layers and, at low tide, you may see fossil ammonites, belemnites and a variety of molluscs embedded in the flat, sea-washed layers. Increasingly, the path gets squeezed between cliff and shore through a landscape of pure theatre. It is a moot point whether the human figures here are spectators or actors. Look up from the path and train your binoculars on the tiers of the cliff and you are very likely to see a stag or wild goat looking down at you as you stand against the backdrop of the sea. The unstable and precipitous cliffs are very free from human disturbance and the creatures that inhabit them feel secure in their terrain. Stop frequently, ply the binoculars and you should see deer and wild goats, perhaps a raven mobbing an eagle or a rabbit skittering away from a peregrine. There is so much to look at that the keen wildlife watcher may never make it to the Arches themselves, but if you do, you will find them colonised by nesting fulmars in the spring and you may be rewarded with the rare sighting of a chough. The Arches, though, bring one back to geology — they were carved out by the sea at a time when the land level was much lower and the sea powered its way through weaknesses in the basalt of which they are formed. A head for heights is needed if you want to go over the top of the first arch to look at the second but it is an exciting climax to this excellent excursion.

Garmony Walk (about 2m)

Start at the car park signposted by Forest Enterprise opposite the rugby pitch 4 miles north of Craignure. Set off across the footbridge towards Fishnish. Walk quietly and keep your eyes and ears open as you follow the level grassy path through low scrub with areas of sedge and marsh, small streams and occasional patches of open water. Look out for vole runs in the grass, mink droppings, and tracks in the mud where deer have crossed the path. There is an abundance of wild flowers on this walk attracting a variety of insects including butterflies such as Scotch Argus. Above fresh water you will see dragonflies and frogs in the marshy ditches. As the path gets closer to the sea, you will see all the common birds of the shore: oyster catchers, curlews, herons, shags and gulls. Terns nest on Grey Isles at the southern entrance to the Sound of Mull and a variety of ducks and divers may be seen offshore. Remember to walk quietly, stopping to look and listen at regular intervals. A scan with the binoculars out to sea might pick up a red-throated diver and a scan of the sky towards the hills a buzzard or even an eagle. Moving on into the trees you will see familiar woodland birds and perhaps a party of long-tailed tits. Once you get to Fishnish there is a heronry in the tall spruces by the picnic area and this is a good place to go otter spotting along the rocky shore, failing that you will almost certainly see a seal.

Postscript

Although you may not believe it, you are already equipped with the most sophisticated apparatus it is possible to own – and it comes completely free. Did you know that human beings can recognise an object that is flashed onto a screen for just one five-hundredth of a second? That means that you already possess the ability to recognise familiar creatures as they dart across your field of vision. You can probably recognise a familiar tune, a make of car, or a person from the same very briefest of clues – sound or shape or movement. Spotting wildlife needs the same degree of familiarity and practice.

We hope this book will show you how to use these skills to understand, find, and most importantly to watch the creatures you want to see. Each day that you practise these skills you will find you are learning amazing things about the way animals behave, where they live, why they live there and sometimes what they do in their homes. You have taken the first steps towards becoming a supreme nature detective – now get out there and enjoy!